INDUSTRIALIZATION
IN INFOGRAPHICS

Enviro Graphics

CHERRY LAKE PRESS

Published in the United States of America by Cherry Lake Publishing Group
Ann Arbor, Michigan
www.cherrylakepublishing.com

Reading Adviser: Marla Conn, MS, Ed., Literacy specialist, Read-Ability, Inc.
Photo Credits: ©Clker-Free-Vector-Images/Pixabay, cover; ©OpenClipart-Vectors/Pixabay, cover; ©Shutterstock, cover; ©Shutterstock, 1; ©Shutterstock, 4; ©Shutterstock, 5; ©ArtsyBee/Pixabay, 6; ©OpenClipart-Vectors/Pixabay, 7; ©AlexZel/Pixabay, 7; ©Shutterstock, 7; ©JCURSEM/Pixabay, 8; ©JerzyGorecki/Pixabay, 8; ©Shutterstock, 8; ©Shutterstock, 9; ©Shutterstock, 11; ©Shutterstock, 14; ©OpenClipart-Vectors/Pixabay, 16; ©Shutterstock, 17; ©Shutterstock, 19; ©Shutterstock, 21; ©Shutterstock, 23; ©Shutterstock, 25; ©Shutterstock, 26; ©BilliTheCat/Pixabay, 28; ©REDQUASAR/Pixabay, 28; ©Shutterstock, 28; ©StarShopping/Pixabay, 29; ©OpenClipart-Vectors/Pixabay, 29; ©Shutterstock, 29; ©ArtMarie/E+/Getty Images, 30

Cherry Lake Press is an imprint of Cherry Lake Publishing Group.

Library of Congress Cataloging-in-Publication Data has been filed and is available at catalog.loc.gov

Cherry Lake Publishing Group would like to acknowledge the work of the
Partnership for 21st Century Learning, a Network of Battelle for Kids. Please
visit http://www.battelleforkids.org/networks/p21 for more information.

Printed in the United States of America
Corporate Graphics

TABLE OF CONTENTS

What Is Industrialization?

Industrialization is when countries start to use machines to do work. The work was first done by hand. Technology makes **production** faster and cheaper. Industrialization changes the average person's life. This includes where they live, the type of work they do, and how much money they make. But it can cause many environmental issues. Pollution and loss of **resources** are two examples. Many countries are trying to balance industrialization with protecting the environment.

BEFORE INDUSTRIALIZATION

| Small shops | In-home businesses | By hand | Slow | Few products | Little **income** |

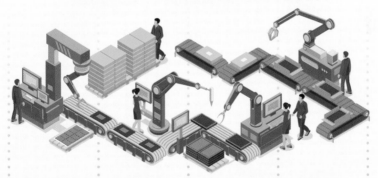

| Large businesses | Factories | Machines | Fast | Many products | A lot of income |

AFTER INDUSTRIALIZATION

CHAPTER 1

The History of Industrialization

Industrialization has not been a steady process. Instead, there have been brief periods of time when things changed quickly. These time periods are called the Industrial Revolutions. The first began in Great Britain in the late 1700s. The second was in the late 1800s and early 1900s. It was focused in the United States.

Early industrialization was driven by production of **textiles**.

In Great Britain, the number of people living in cities rose from **15% TO 85%**.

Coal production grew by **500%** in Great Britain.

Production moved from homes to factories.

People living in U.S. cities went from **6% TO 40%**.

Railroad lines grew from **35,000 MILES* TO 254,000 MILES** in just 51 years in the United States.

New technology led to mass production.

Large factories and companies were created.

*1 mile = 1.6 kilometers

TECHNOLOGY PROFILES

1793: COTTON GIN

- Eli Whitney invents the cotton gin, a machine that removes seeds from cotton.
- The United States provides an estimated 2/3 of the world's cotton supply by 1860.
- Before, it took a lot of time to remove seeds. After, cotton could be harvested in half the time.

1769: STEAM ENGINE

- James Watt makes improvements to the steam engine.
- Watt also coins the term "horsepower."
- Before, factories had to be next to a river to use waterpower. After, factories could be anywhere.

1879: POLLUTION REDUCTION

- Mary Walton **patents** a device. It moves smoke from factories into water tanks, then into the sewage system.
- Walton also invents a system for noise pollution. It can be used for loud train cars.
- Before, New York City, New York, was becoming very polluted. After, Walton's work inspired others to clean up the effects of industrialization.

BOOK PRODUCTION OVER TIME

0.007
books
per day

2.5
books
per day

25
books
per day

THOUSANDS
of e-books
per day

Scribes

**First Printing
Press**

**Steam-Powered
Printing**

Internet

2019, Our World in Data

CHAPTER 2

Industrialization Today

Today, many countries are industrialized. Others have yet to go through their own industrial revolutions. A country changes dramatically with industrialization, as do the lives of its people. China and India are examples of newly industrialized countries. Their **gross domestic product** (GDP) increases as they develop more and more.

COMMON JOBS

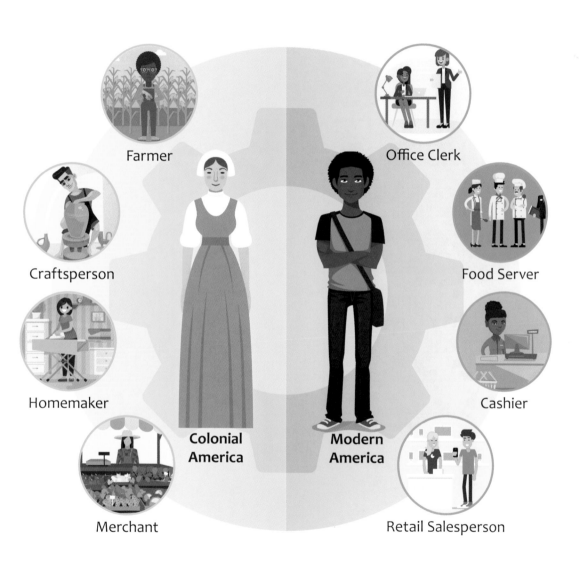

Farmer

Craftsperson

Homemaker

Merchant

Colonial America

Modern America

Office Clerk

Food Server

Cashier

Retail Salesperson

PERIODS OF INDUSTRIALIZATION

MID-1800S–LATE 1800S

Canada
Australia
European countries

LATE 1700S–EARLY 1800S

Great Britain
France
Belgium
The German states
United States

[21ST CENTURY SKILLS LIBRARY]

1900S–PRESENT

Asia
Africa
Latin America

AVERAGE ANNUAL INCOME

Highly industrialized

Switzerland **$83,580**

United States **$62,850**

Newly industrialized

Brazil **$9,140**

Thailand **$6,610**

Not industrialized

Afghanistan **$550**

Democratic Republic of the Congo **$490**

2019, Our World in Data

CITY GROWTH OVER TIME

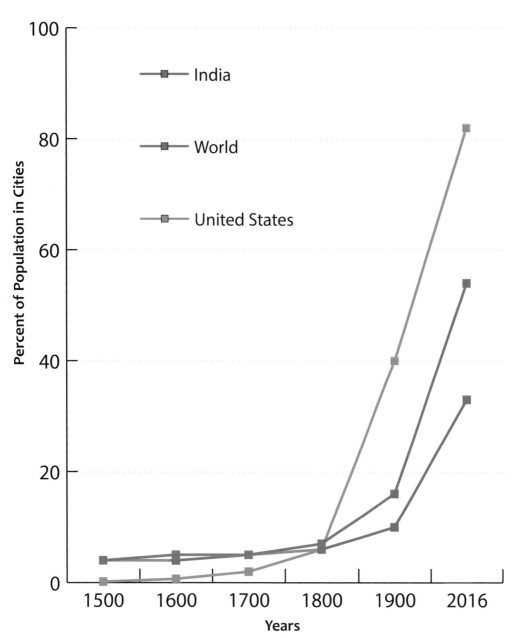

2019, Our World in Data

CHAPTER 3

Environmental Issues

As countries become industrialized, they use more resources. This includes fossil fuels, such as oil and coal. It takes millions of years to make fossil fuels. Industrialized countries use them up very quickly. Industry also creates pollution. This pollution can spoil Earth's air, water, and soil, as well as living things.

RESOURCE USE BY COUNTRY

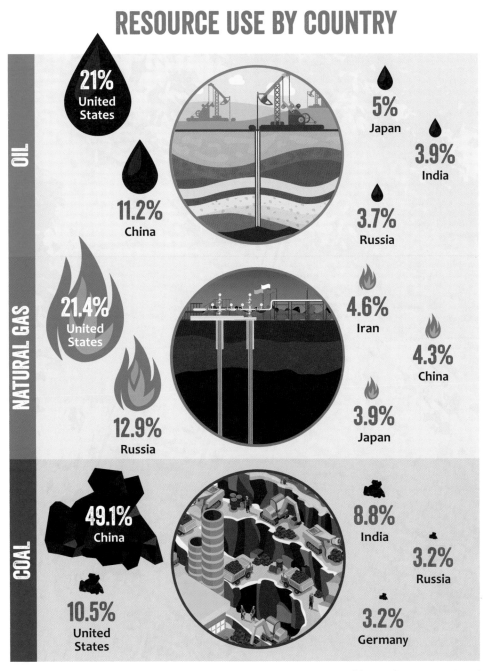

OIL

21%
United States

11.2%
China

5%
Japan

3.9%
India

3.7%
Russia

NATURAL GAS

21.4%
United States

12.9%
Russia

4.6%
Iran

4.3%
China

3.9%
Japan

COAL

49.1%
China

10.5%
United States

8.8%
India

3.2%
Russia

3.2%
Germany

2014, Public Radio International

AIR POLLUTION

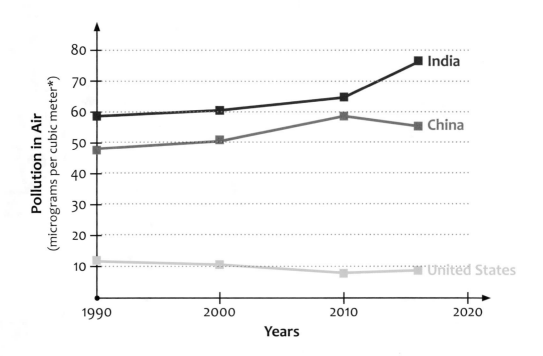

*1 cubic meter = 1.3 cubic yards

2017, Our World in Data

AIR POLLUTION EXPOSURE

2019, Our World in Data

GLOBAL SOURCES OF WATER POLLUTION

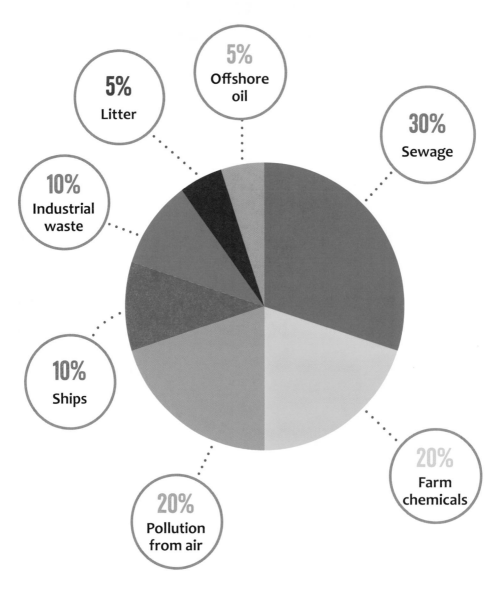

5%
Offshore oil

5%
Litter

30%
Sewage

10%
Industrial waste

10%
Ships

20%
Farm chemicals

20%
Pollution from air

2015, Information for Action

[21ST CENTURY SKILLS LIBRARY]

WATER POLLUTION FACTS

Each year, an estimated
1.4 MILLION TONS
of oil are released into
the sea.

8 MILLION TONS
of plastic have been
dumped into the world's
oceans every year
since 2015.

2 MILLION TONS
of sewage and waste are
dumped into water
each day.

2018 Water Logic; 2015 National Geographic; 2002 U.S. National Academy of Sciences

GLOBAL SOURCES OF LAND POLLUTION

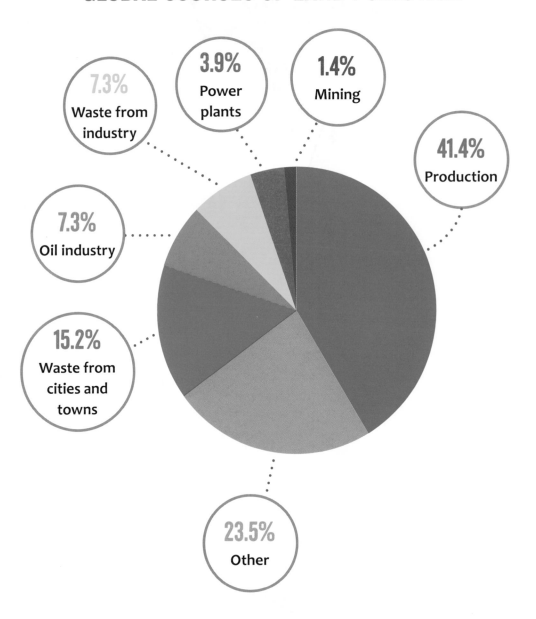

7.3% Waste from industry

3.9% Power plants

1.4% Mining

41.4% Production

7.3% Oil industry

15.2% Waste from cities and towns

23.5% Other

2018, Handbook of Environmental Materials Management

LAND POLLUTION FACTS

1/3 of the land on Earth is severely **degraded** by industrialization.

16% of the soil in China is polluted.

There are more than **1,300** sites on the United States' top list of places with dangerous soil pollution.

2018 Food and Agriculture Organization of the United Nations (UN); 2017 UN Convention to Combat Desertification

LAND USE OVER TIME

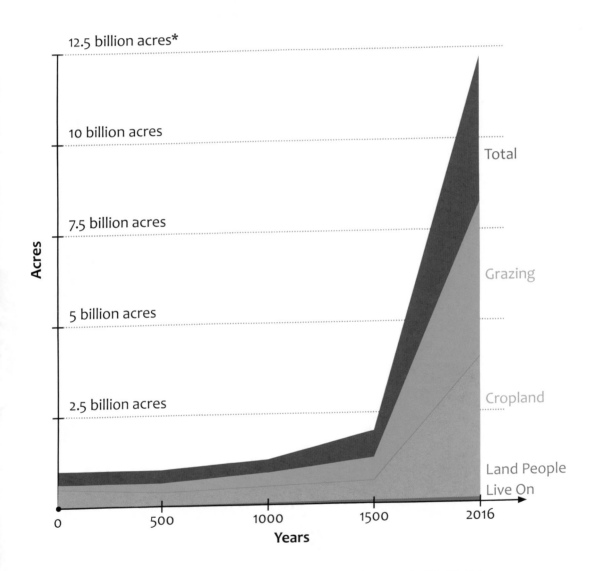

*1 acre = 0.4 hectare

2019, Our World in Data

HUMAN ISSUES

Diseases of **Affluence**
The number of
Americans with
DIABETES doubled
between 1999
and 2019.

Pollution
Air pollution is linked
to
6.5 MILLION deaths.

Overcrowding
In 2019, 55% of the world lived
in cities. This might be **68%**
by 2050.

Food Shortages
As of 2017, **1 IN 8**
Americans experience
hunger and
food insecurity.

CHAPTER 4

Solutions

There are many ways to reduce the negative impacts of industrialization. People have worked hard to change laws. There are many steps people can take in their daily lives too.

SOLUTION 1

Reduce the use of products that cause pollution.

💡 **Success story** – *Lead was used in gasoline. It was removed from gasoline in the 1970s. Then, much less lead polluted the environment.*

SOLUTION 2

Treat industrial waste to remove **toxins**.

💡 **Success story** – *Factories dumped waste right into the Ohio River. It was very polluted and unsafe. In the 1940s, states came together. Laws were passed to keep the river clean of toxins.*

PROBLEM
Industrial pollution

SOLUTION 1

Reduce the amount of pollution that leaks into **groundwater**.

💡 **Success story** – *Cities and towns gather waste in landfills. Before the 1980s, leaks from this waste went right into the groundwater. Since then, landfills have been lined with a layer of plastic to prevent leaks.*

SOLUTION 2

Reduce the amount of plastic in the world's oceans.

💡 **Success story** – *The Ocean Cleanup project has a goal to clean up 90 percent of plastic pollution. It is working to prevent plastic litter by stopping it at rivers. Litter is also being removed from the ocean.*

PROBLEM
Water pollution

WHAT YOU CAN DO TO HELP

Reduce waste

Pick up litter when you see it.

Reduce consumption

Find ways around the house to reduce energy use. Turn off lights and unplug electronics.

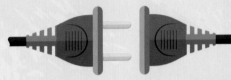

Reduce food waste

Plan meals to avoid buying too much food.

Restore some habitat

Plant native plants around your home.

Reach out to lawmakers

Anyone can call, email, or send a letter to their local lawmakers.

[21ST CENTURY SKILLS LIBRARY]

Put a trash bag in
each car.

Reuse or **repurpose**
plastic waste.

Walk and bike more, carpool,
and ride the bus.

Use less water
at home.

Take home and eat
restaurant leftovers.

Donate
unwanted
food.

Volunteer with a local
restoration group.

Explain your concerns
and how you think the
lawmakers can help.

Send a thank-you
note if they vote to
help your issue.

REDUCE SINGLE-USE PLASTICS

There are many ways to help with pollution. One is to reduce your consumption of single-use plastics.

1. For 3 days, keep a log of the single-use plastics you use and throw away. This might include plastic bags, straws, and water bottles.

2. Take stock of single-use plastics in your home. Do an inventory for each room. What plastic bottles, tubs, and bags will eventually get thrown away? Ask your teacher if you can do the same for your classroom.

3. Review your list. Brainstorm ways to reuse or repurpose each item. Which items could be replaced with longer-lasting alternatives?

Learn More

BOOKS

Labrecque, Ellen. *Recycling and Waste.* Ann Arbor, MI: Cherry Lake Publishing, 2018.

Litmanovich, Ellina. *Real-World Projects to Explore the Industrial Revolution.* New York, NY: Rosen Central, 2019.

Lynch, Seth. *The Industrial Revolution.* New York, NY: Gareth Stevens Publishing, 2018.

WEBSITES

Fossil Fuels
https://www.studentenergy.org/topics/fossil-fuels

Industrial Revolution Inventions
www.american-historama.org/industrial-revolution-inventions.htm

Kids Environment Kids Health
https://kids.niehs.nih.gov/topics/index.htm

BIBLIOGRAPHY

Bomboy, Scott. National Constitution Center. "The Cotton Gin: A Game-Changing Social and Economic Invention." Last modified March 14, 2019. https://constitutioncenter.org/blog/the-cotton-gin-a-game-changing-social-and-economic-invention

Ritchie, Hannah. Our World in Data. "How Long Before We Run Out of Fossil Fuels?" Last modified August 08, 2017. https://ourworldindata.org/how-long-before-we-run-out-of-fossil-fuels

U.S. Bureau of Labor Statistics. "Occupational Employment Statistics." Last modified May 2018. https://www.bls.gov/oes/current/area_emp_chart/area_emp_chart_data.htm#United%20States

World Data. "Average Income around the World." https://www.worlddata.info/average-income.php

GLOSSARY

affluence (AF-loo-ens) wealth

degraded (dih-GRAY-ded) broken down or damaged

gross domestic product (GROHSS duh-MES-tik PRAH-dukt) the value of a country's goods and services produced in one year

groundwater (GROWND-wah-tur) water that collects and flows underground

income (IN-kum) money that is regularly gained from doing work

patents (PAT-ents) obtains the legal right to be the only one to make and sell a certain product

production (pruh-DUHK-shun) the process of making items for sale or use

repurpose (ree-PURP-ess) to use something for a different purpose

resources (REE-sor-sez) materials, such as oil, that a country has and can use to increase its wealth

textile (TEK-stile) a fabric that is usually woven or knit

toxins (TOK-sinz) poisonous materials that can affect the health of living things

INDEX

ABOUT THE AUTHOR

Renae Gilles is an author, editor, and ecologist from the Pacific Northwest. She has a bachelor's degree in humanities from Evergreen State College and a master's in biology from Eastern Washington University. Renae and her husband live in Washington with their two daughters, Edith and Louisa.